POSTMODERN ENCOUNTERS

Umberto Eco and Football

Peter Pericles Trifonas

Series editor: Richard Appignanesi

ICON BOOKS UK

TOTEM BOOKS USA

Published in the UK in 2001
by Icon Books Ltd., Grange Road,
Duxford, Cambridge CB2 4QF
E-mail: info@iconbooks.co.uk
www.iconbooks.co.uk

Published in the USA in 2001
by Totem Books
Inquiries to: Icon Books Ltd.,
Grange Road, Duxford,
Cambridge CB2 4QF, UK

Sold in the UK, Europe, South Africa
and Asia by Faber and Faber Ltd.,
3 Queen Square, London WC1N 3AU
or their agents

Distributed to the trade in the USA by
National Book Network Inc.,
4720 Boston Way, Lanham,
Maryland 20706

Distributed in the UK, Europe,
South Africa and Asia by
Macmillan Distribution Ltd.,
Houndmills, Basingstoke RG21 6XS

Distributed in Canada by
Penguin Books Canada,
10 Alcorn Avenue, Suite 300,
Toronto, Ontario M4V 3B2

Published in Australia in 2001
by Allen & Unwin Pty. Ltd.,
83 Alexander Street,
Crows Nest, NSW 2065

Text copyright © 2001 Peter Pericles Trifonas

The author has asserted his moral rights.

Series editor: Richard Appignanesi

ISBN 1 84046 280 9

Typesetting by Wayzgoose

Printed and bound in the UK by
Cox & Wyman Ltd., Reading

*To Effie for helping me not
to forget how,*

*'Life is like a mirror, it takes
the reflection of signs and gives them
the tain of wonder.'*

Before Football ... There Was the Sign

The laws of signification are the laws of culture.[1]
Umberto Eco

The culture industry runs sign systems rampant. The projections of its media exact immeasurable influence on minds young and not so young. It does not discriminate between those possessing innocence and those wanting knowledge in the age of consumer-orientated global economies in which the desire for instant gratification is driven by the digital mantra of the day. The culture industry treats the psyche of the neophyte and the mature reader of cultural phenomena equally – with the same amount of impersonal discourtesy when it comes to arbitrarily evaluating, sorting and commodifying the signs of culture through the media and its simulations of reality. To yoke ethics with representational concerns is only natural for critical readers of culture. Criticality is paramount for Umberto Eco, whose work in semiotics aims at raising human consciousness towards the

5

effects of signs upon our everyday practices of making meaning *in* and *of* the life-world. Especially, if we consider a sign to be an image or a text that we learn through, about and from.

For those who participate in and run the culture industry, it is a means of focusing and obsessing subjective desire in an economy of intellectual and material self-fulfilment based on an empire of signs whose terms and values are to be worked out and actualised at any and all costs. As Eco has pointed out, a sign has no analogous, motivational or correlational link with what it represents in reality, because it is arbitrarily produced and mediates for our understanding of reality.[2] A sign is an *interpretant* (see 'Key Ideas and Glossary' at the end of this book) of experience, an idiosyncratically constructed mental tool used to reference and understand the world. The sign is all surface, all projection, all image: complete in itself and for itself. Thus, it has a directive force of its own that defies the reciprocity of a two-way model of communication. It sends the logic of itself and attempts to make plain its *raison d'être* for all to see – or perhaps to miss. It *re*-presents information and dissimulates reality through its power to initiate and sustain a form of symbolic violence upon those who engage in, create and apprehend the values of the sign as a model of reality. That is, the semiotic force of its re-presentation of information enhances the effects of its message as the effects of the sign are internalised by the viewer/consumer of the image. The viewer/consumer cannot alter the form of the sign, but only imbibe and complete its intentionality by aesthetic and cognitive, conscious and unconscious responses in relation to the image. On the one hand, the sign in itself is therefore intransitory, both subject and object, and needs no mediative completion by way of a subjective predicate that puts its meaning into action. It suffices as the symbolic representation of meaning itself. On the other hand, the sign is its own pedagogy; it teaches, but it needs a viewer/consumer to fulfil the intentional and extentional limits of its communicative potential as a meaning-making tool.

So, what does the sign of 'football' signify? What does it promise? What does it fulfil in culture? What are the sources and openings of the real and symbolic violence of football? Its pedagogy? If, indeed, football has a teaching. How does it inform subjectivity and the living text of cultural and social practices? How can we engage the real and symbolic violence of the sign of football?

Umberto Eco addresses like-minded questions in his cultural criticism – of course, not always in relation to football. His interest in it is complementary to his overall semiotic inquiry and informed thoroughly by it. How semiotics works is not clearly spelled out in such texts, so as not to assail the general reader with theoretical abstraction. When Eco writes as a cultural critic, he provides intellectual and emotional insight on various aspects of everyday life by undertaking, more or less, case studies of difficult and puzzling situations that cause him to reflect on the logic of existing social structures, values and artefacts. The subjects are diverse and eclectic: how to recognise a pornographic film; using a fax machine; obtaining a driver's licence; bad coffee; student revolts; fakes and forgeries; Marshall McLuhan; computers; Disneyland; James Bond movies; comic book characters such as Superman; playing the recorder. To read Eco the cultural critic is to be immersed in the excesses of culture. Parody always comes first.

Umberto Eco and Football is therefore neither about Umberto Eco the football fan, nor about Umberto Eco the semiotics theorist – nor even about Umberto Eco the novelist – as much as it is about the way in which the diversity of Eco's work as a public intellectual and cultural theorist allows us to engage in readings of the trepidation, concerns and follies that we experience in everyday life. In this respect, football is both a metaphor and a motif for engaging the intellectual meanderings of a writer and thinker on the subject of culture. It offers a way into analysing the jarring elements of a wide-ranging textual corpus which comments on the ways in which traditions and ideals are communicated, mobilised, obsessed over and acted out in our own public and private possible worlds.

Like all postmodern encounters, *Umberto Eco and Football* therefore *is* and *is not* a text about Eco and football. There are more hermeneutical layers at work here, beyond the recognisable notational markers denoting an individual and the world's most popular game that constitute the subjects of its title. Not to mention the evocative collage of the cover of the text, with its visual representations that rely, yet play, on the spectacle of football and the cult of personality that focuses the media's merciless obsession on the lives of high-profile players such as David Beckham and Eric Cantona because 'the fans want to know and have the right to know'.

I want to make something clear to the reader from the start. Football is merely one vehicle among many others that enable Umberto Eco to read the nuances and the excesses of human actions in the name of culture, to critically engage a plethora of topics in his creative and scholarly work – be it the psychological sources of our fascination with sport and celebrity, presenting serendipitous misreadings of great books like the Bible that are the pillars of Western culture, positing the existence of an Aristotelian text on the poetics of comedy and weaving a detective story around this hypothesis, speculating on ancient conspiracies involving the occult, or simply narrating a cautionary tale about the perils of travelling with a large smoked salmon. We must keep this firmly in mind.

Football, in this sense, is a sign that leads to other signs and back again in quite arbitrary and surprising ways. The image that Eco likes to use is the rhizome or the labyrinth, a trap of openings and closures in which conjecture and infinite possibility rule over certainty and structure to destabilise the notion of a fixed truth waiting somewhere out there to be discovered.[3] Like Umberto Eco, we will at times stray quite far afield from football, clinging to it by what may seem to be only the thinnest of metonymical chains. Yet if we rattle one link in the chain, it goes on to affect the others, until all are vibrating with kinetic energy. So, let the reader be forewarned. Eco would say – and has said in the postscript to *The Name of the Rose* – that every act of reading has its price to pay, a penance perhaps for the sublime nature of the experience. The reader who wants to gain entrance into the possible worlds of the text, in the quest for the knowledge of a truth, may arrive only at the ephemeral and transitory at best.

Semiotics, Culture and Football

Perhaps it would be best to engage in fewer political discussions and more circenses *sociology. Is it possible to have a revolution on a football Sunday?*[4]   Umberto Eco

Umberto Eco seems to revel in the carnivalesque of popular culture, its semiotic by-products and communication practices. The mundane minutiae of everyday life have not traditionally been a topic of analysis for so-called 'serious intellectuals', who have upheld the reason for establishing an imaginary dividing line between academic life and public life with remarkable tenacity. A semiotic theorist of international reputation, Eco was doing 'cultural studies' when the implications of the field had neither been conceived nor conceptualised in disciplinary terms. From 1954 to 1959, he worked as a cultural editor for RAI, Italian Radio-Television. Since the 1950s, when his academic and literary career began, Eco has also contributed regularly to daily newspapers (*Corriere della Sera*), weekly magazines (*L'Espresso*) and artistic and intellectual periodicals (*Quindici, Il Verri*). This is telling when we consider that the study of culture has only been legitimised and justified outside the fields of anthropology, history and sociology and their formalised methodological apparatuses within the last twenty-five years. As a semiotician, novelist and cultural critic, Eco has broken epistemological ground and tested intellectual boundaries by addressing the signifying potential and implications of everyday life experiences. Signs, images, events and occurrences orientate human beings and bring about certain attitudes and behaviours. Semiotics makes it possible at least to try to understand how and why.

So, it could be said that for Eco the world is a text in which all signs are perpetually 'in play'. Signs are able to proliferate both in their associations and in the way in which they deviate from their sources. That makes signs equal in their ability to signify and to lie or deviate from the truth. Eco explains:

Semiotics is concerned with everything that can be taken *as a sign. A sign is everything which can be taken as significantly substituting for something else. This something else does not necessarily have to exist or actually be somewhere at the moment in which a sign stands for it. Thus,* semiotics is in principle the discipline studying everything which can be used in order to lie. *If something cannot be used to tell a lie, conversely it cannot be used to tell the truth; it cannot in fact be used 'to tell' at all. I think that the definition of a 'theory of the lie' should be taken as a pretty comprehensive program for a general semiotics.*[5]

Football is one of these signs, among others, based on a lie. It cannibalises and carnivalises culture – uses its systems of representation according to its own arbitrary rules – to make it play a game of make-believe that is taken quite seriously and sometimes has grave consequences. The implications of this hypothesis will be evident soon enough. Suffice to say that games are not real life and should not be taken as such, or so the story goes. It becomes quite necessary then to ask: *Why does football arouse powerful displays of emotion if it is only a game? Why do people live and die for it?*

Ludi Circenses: Reading Football

There is one thing that – even if it were considered essential – no student movement or urban revolt or global protest or what have you would ever be able to do. And that is to occupy the football field on a Sunday.[6]

Umberto Eco

Umberto Eco reads football as a neurosis of culture. It is a manifestation of something gone awry in the human psyche for which there is neither a reasonable explanation nor an effective cure. For those who are stricken by its debilitating effects, there is no definitive treatment, no painless therapy or intervention to be worked through; there is only the endless suffering of watching the exquisite *agon* of the game that takes place on the field every football Sunday. Such is the joy and the curse of the football fan. The irony is that the punishment is self-inflicted. Or is it? The hypothesis of football as a psychopathology of repressed desire is one that Eco revels in:

... the spectators – the majority, that is – who, in fact, behave like hordes of sex maniacs regularly going to see (not once in their lifetime in Amsterdam but every Sunday, and instead of) couples making love, or pretending to (something like the very poor children of my childhood, who were promised they would be taken to watch the rich eating ice cream).[7]

It is quite easy to use the Freudian theory of obsessive compulsive behaviour and voyeurism to characterise the on-going psychic state of the stereotypical football fan. Each and every Sunday, as Eco tells us, the stadiums will be bursting with bodies for no other reason than simply that there is a game on. Like the seemingly illogical fascination of the child, observed by Freud, playing alone with a spinning top in the absence of the mother and saying *fort/da* to himself with great anticipation while watching it go forward and come back, the football fan is doomed to repeat past experience. There is no choice – not a *conscious* one at least, as the subconscious works itself out on the football field and in the stadium.

The repetition compulsion is what Freud calls the need to fill the void of the loss of meaning provided by the absence of the mother, who of course stands for all that is good and wholesome in the child's world. In fact, the mother *is* the child's world, satiating all wants and needs. Like the motherless child who needs to substitute the anxiety of that loss with the full presence of the top, upon which all emotion – grief and joy – is transferred in an infinite plenitude, the football fan needs and craves football. There is no substitute. Not an obvious one, anyway. This Freudian theory grounds the point that Eco is making about the motivation of football fans (although I must admit that I have taken great happiness in putting forward the case!).

But here is the kicker. Besides being an obsessive compulsive, the football fan as spectator and not participant in the game itself is even worse off than Freud's poor child, because the fan's relationship with football is second-hand and consequently voyeuristic. The incapacity for performance (libidinal pun intended) motivates the need for the vicarious thrill of spectating so as to try to stimulate – subliminally and physically – the release of (sexual) anxiety via engaging in a form of visual pleasure that affects the body. The spectatorly focus on the game is therefore a transitive experience – utterly incomplete in itself and, in the end, unsatisfying – and it becomes a visually based type of substitute that seeks to replace the real experience of actually playing the game, but never does. Thus, the football fan must have football every football Sunday like the frustrated sex maniacs that Eco describes. Of course, we can use Freudian psychology to analyse the spectatorship of other sports fans, and we could very well come to similar conclusions. It therefore becomes necessary to look at specific cases to test the theory within 'the football imagination'. And there is not just one overriding mentality.

If we begin to look at the chants and songs used by various supporters of football clubs at local, regional or national levels, there are some less than savoury implications when we consider, in a Freudian light, the radical edge of the list of themes covered. For example, how could we possibly explain the fact that the Aberdeen fans are taunted by the chant, 'Sheepshagging bastards, you're only'? Even more worrisome, from a psychoanalytic viewpoint, is the fact that those same Aberdeen fans have welcomed this hackneyed characterisation of themselves and their sexual peccadillos and have used it as a rallying cry to turn the tables on opposing fans by answering back, 'Sheep-shagging bastards, we're only'.[8] At some point, it becomes necessary to engage Umberto Eco's semiotic theory head on, which is a difficult thing to do at the best of times. Now is as good a time as any. Using Eco's notion of codic manipulation, we can explain the co-optation of this most specious of epithets by the more dedicated Aberdeen fans as an example of active ideological code switching, or intention-ally playing the ideology of the terms of defini-tion against itself and against the accepted parameters of the interpretative code that ren-der the slogan 'Sheepshagging bastards, you're only' as ultimately bizarre and derogatory.[9] The ideological code switching that the Aberdeen fans manage to pull off is done by displacing the negative emotional connotations of the chant and infusing it with a positive charge towards which the terms of representa-tion, now redefined, work to concretise the dis-tinctive and recognisable football identity of the most dedicated of Aberdeen fans via an appeal to the sexually grotesque and absurd.

A football identity is not a 'real' or empirical identity, but a way effectively to differentiate between football identities opposed within the cultural carnival of football, in which the ethical and moral bounds of all normality are suspended for the purpose of rooting on a team and showing fan support. Insults, physical challenges, visual provocations, obscene gestures and references – including ritualistic behaviour – are nothing new to the rivalry surrounding the expression of fanhood. They will never disappear as long as an ethos of competition thrives to orientate the emotions of the spectators and allow them to map out football identities in relation to team allegiances that pose one group against its 'others'. Interestingly enough, the Aberdeen football club attempted to defuse the disturbing fan appeal of the 'sheepshagger' image and summarily introduced a new mascot, 'Angus the Bull', to try to redirect the focus of the fans and thereby to rehabilitate the animalistic theme of the carnival atmosphere encircling the team. Thus far, the results have been mixed.

Homo Sportivus

According to Eco, 'Sport is Man, Sport is Society'.[10] The capitalisation of the words signifies the canonical seriousness of the statement and establishes the extent of its historicity. In itself, the statement is perhaps *the* cultural edict of Western civilisation that Eco construes as a *principle of being* beyond question. He calls the source of this unspoken mental connection of sport, humanity and society, the 'deep area of the collective sensibility'.[11] The logic of the associations conjoining and legitimating the truth of these words and what concepts they convey is rooted in the historical specificity of the cultural memory that is the 'Maximum Cement'[12] of the social sphere in the West. Breaking the bonds between sport, humanity and society and the practices they signify would cause 'a crisis in every possible associative principle'[13] arising from them, and reveal 'what is not human in the relationship of sociality'.[14] This, it would seem, is Eco's secret hope: to break the logic of the syntagmatic chain – those semantic relations and inter-relations – conceptually linking sport, humanity and society, as it is articulated by and through the fanaticism surrounding the game of football; not to mention the paraphernalia (scarves, flags, pins, etc.) and the ritualistic practices that govern the world of football fandom and strengthen the ties that bind and separate human beings from each other in relation to club allegiances. For the salvation of society itself, it would seem that Eco must expose football for what it is: only a game and not a way of life. Otherwise, humanity will continue to suffer in the meantime at the hands of those who manipulate the representation of the game and use it as a form of social control.

But the reason is also personal, as Eco admits in 'The World Cup and its Pomps':

Many malignant readers, seeing how I discuss here the noble sport of football with detachment, irritation, and (oh, all right) malevolence, will harbour the vulgar suspicion that I don't love football because football has never loved me, for from my earliest childhood I belonged to that category of infants and adolescents who, the moment they kick the ball – assuming that they manage to kick it – promptly send it into their own goal or, at best, pass it to the opponent, unless with stubborn tenacity they send it off the field, beyond hedges and fences, to become lost in a basement or stream or to plunge among the flavours of the ice cream cart. And so his playmates reject him and banish him from the happiest of competitive events. And no suspicion will ever be more patently true.[15]

Football, if we are to believe him, made Eco feel inadequate among his childhood peers. There is nothing like ineptness at sport and the resulting exile into the world of bookish things to create a man of letters. Eco explains that despite the efforts of his father – 'a sober but loyal fan' who took him to football matches[16] – he began to associate the game with 'a cosmic meaningless performance'[17] that eventually manifested itself via reflection on the uncanniness of the experience of everyday reality into more meaningful and dire questions concerning theology and the meaning of life. Football proves to be an unexpected catalyst for a crisis of faith that Eco confesses he had: '[F]or the first time I doubted the existence of God and decided that the world was a pointless fiction.'[18] Driven to consulting a 'wise Capuchin'[19] for advice about the state of his soul, Eco the younger was given strong reasons for conserving his belief in God, 'because reliable people like Dante, Newton, Manzoni, T. S. Eliot, and Pat Boone had believed in God without the slightest difficulty'.[20] All this for the sake of being a mediocre football player in the early stages of life. How can we believe it?

Eco confirms the curious nature of his conceptualisation of the game and its effects on his psyche and soul:

... I have been telling all this to indicate how, as far back as I can remember, football for me

has been linked with the absence of purpose and the vanity of all things, and the fact that the Supreme Being may be (or may not be) simply a hole. And perhaps for this reason I (alone, I think, among all living creatures) have always associated the game of football with negative philosophies.[21]

Mind you, Eco uses a great deal of exaggeration and parodic 'what ifs' to state the case against football as he begins to chip away at the cultural myth of *Homo sportivus*. This humorous dimension of analysis by way of the well-worn rhetorical device that we might call 'the public confession of the intellectual' constitutes the obligatory sugar-coating of the pill. We must take it at face value that Eco is thoroughly surprised that he of all people should be asked by the editors of *L'Espresso* – whom he assumes are suffering from 'an excess of metaphysical vertigo'[22] – to discuss the World Cup. The story is either too outlandish not to be truthful, or at least a well constructed lie, too good not to be believed, as Eco's theory of semiotics would have it.

No matter how funny or absurd it seems, we cannot ignore the validity of Eco's message about the social risks and dangers of a fanatical interest in the game of football. History has shown us that this is only too true. If we look at the Heysel Stadium tragedy[23] and the campaigns of violence that are intentionally fought for the sake of supporting an imaginary football identity and the logic of its culture, then we must admit that the game of football has at times taken on disturbing real life consequences in the material transition from carnival spectacle to a vulgar form of cultural expression. Ritual too often begins to supersede the logic of reflection and thought, and no mind is paid to the aftermath of supporting one team over another at all costs. Violence seems required to show the extent of one's allegiance to, and passion for, a fictitious identity born of a game. Admittedly, the social and cultural dynamics of fanaticism are more complex. Violence does not always accompany football. Eco concedes that there is some merit in encouraging the release of pent-up emotions allowed by the circus atmosphere of the stadium, given that we know exactly what ethical purposes it serves and why. Again, his analysis is wry and cutting, evoking the spectatorly lure of high-risk activities and sports to characterise the sickly nature of the fanatical ethos of a possible world in which the organised violence of football could be construed as desirable and even useful:

I am in favour of football passion as I am in favour of drag racing, of competition between motorcycles on the edge of a cliff, and of wild parachute jumping, mystical mountain climbing, crossing oceans in rubber dinghies, Russian roulette, and the use of narcotics. Races improve the race, and all these games lead fortunately to the death of the best, allowing mankind to continue its existence serenely with normal protagonists, of underachievement. In a certain sense I could agree with the Futurists that war is the only hygiene of the world, except for one little correction: It would be, if only volunteers were allowed to wage it. Unfortunately war also involves the reluctant, and therefore it is morally inferior to spectator sports.[24]

Eco equates the passion of football with the desire to watch or even participate in entertainments rife with the threat of danger that have the potential to fulfil the proverbial Freudian death wish. The analogy is telling because it speaks of the need of a society and its members to indulge in the folly of experiencing self-destructive pursuits in the name of sports. We could call the events accompanying the game of football 'war' in some cases where the desire for inflicting violence supersedes the goals of the sport and its spectatorship – if by 'war' we mean a human pursuit that has as its primary focus the suspension of all ethical behaviour and any semblance of moral order for the sole purpose of either maiming or killing the other. Eco's analogy is not difficult to take seriously. The metaphors linking football with war occupy the popular vernacular and have empirical validity in that 'skirmishes' and other such 'minor wars' have been fought by hooligan supporters for the sake of the game. Eco never-theless has tongue firmly planted in cheek. He loves 'dangerous' games (like football), he says, because they possess the propensity to cleanse humanity of one of its scourges – *Homo sportivus*, the athletic overachiever – thus leaving ordinary people to populate the earth in anonymous mediocrity.

Making an oblique allusion to football as *ludi circenses* or circus games – most notably, those of the Roman gladiatorial spectacle of the Circus Maximus – Eco is playing on the historical roots of the sport in the spectacle of festivity, debauchery and usurpation that is the celebratory aftermath of war. The first recorded game was on Shrove Tuesday in AD 217, in what is now Derby, England. 'Football' was played as part of a festival to celebrate a deci-sive military victory over a Roman garrison. By the year 1175, the Shrove Tuesday football match was an annual event. Later, the advent of rugby circa 1823 brought about a confusion of nomenclature between the games, and the name 'soccer' – an abbreviation of 'association football' – originated with the formation of the London Football Association (1863) to promote the game that emphasised the kicking of the ball into a goal. Most of the modern forms of football are adapted from ancient games, for example, *harpaston* and *harpastrum*, played in Greece and Rome. These games are seen today in Tuscany and Florence under the moniker of *calcio*, which is also what football is called in Italy today.

Using football as a concrete symbol for the decline of Western civilisation via *circenses*, Eco strikes at the heart of Classical Humanism, which he describes as founded on 'Greek anthropolalia',[25] or the capacity for reason tied to the human animal's power of speech …

… founded in turn not only on contemplation, the notion of the city or the primacy of Doing, but on sport as calculated waste, as masking of the problem, 'chatter' raised to the rank of tumour … sport is the maximum aberration of 'phatic' speech and therefore, finally, the negation of all speech, and hence the beginning

of the dehumanization of man or the 'humanis-
tic' invention of an idea of Man that is decep-
tive at the outset.[26]

Sport dehumanises Man. And it has to be Man,
not wo/man, if we are bringing Classical
Humanism into the mix, since the Greek
anthropos signifies masculine dominance as
the characteristic feature of civil society at the
time of the Golden Age of Greece and the
experiment of democracy – government for and
by the people. For Eco, 'the raising of human
beings dedicated to competition'[27] exemplifies
the violation of nature and the metamorphosis
of athlete to monster – an instrument perfectly
able to execute a series of pre-coded commands.
This castigation may sound severe or even
inappropriate. The thought of sports as a cor-
rupting influence on the authenticity of human
being is shocking to say the least. Eco, of course,
knows this and even depends upon it for
generating certain extentional responses in the
reader trying to grapple with the suggestion.
Sport is supposed to be good. Football is a

sport; therefore, football is good. The end. But the syllogism does not stop there for Eco. It begins again. This time, however, it must start with a reconsideration of what grounds the turn of logic governing the representation of the game as a sport and its underlying concepts. And to this we will now turn.

Toward a Semiogenesis of Football Fanatics

What Eco describes as 'football' is not simply a sport but a type of *semiotic guerrilla warfare*. The signifying systems that encircle the game construct the symbolic field of fandom by communicating an economy of values to participants and spectators through media representations. The sign-forms produced evoke positive and negative valences: some properties of each are *blown up* and others are *narcotised*, depending on the content of the message to be conveyed.[28] Whether it be a high-flying header that sails into the back of the net, a jack-knifing scissor kick in which the player sacrifices his body for a shot on goal, a punishing tackle that leaves the opponent writhing in pain, or the epiphanic penalty kick where the goalie is left to the mercy of an expert marksman shooting the ball at mind-boggling speeds, the images of football being played are not innocent representations of the game. The media apparatus – lexical and visual – actively frames the way in which the signs of football are perceived. Signs are constructed to aim at affectively motivated responses. We might say that they are intentionally directed to achieve an ideal of 'responsiveness' (e.g., surprise, suspense, drama, disgust, joy and so on) whereby emotive associations are piqued. So none of the images of the game – whether experienced live or second-hand – can be accessed purely, that is, in and of themselves without the ideological predisposition of the spectator being affected by media intervention or socially constructed responses. Fanzines and tabloids, advertising campaigns and football chat shows have made sports idols and celebrities of players. Reality takes a back seat to the myth-making of a well-crafted persona developed solely for public consumption. The attitudes towards players fostered within and by fans through the representations of football-related media cannot be totally cleaved from the experience of the game. For example, teams have become human billboards for advertising consumer goods conveniently sold in stadiums. It is not hard to see how an emotional attachment by a fan to a club could translate into a purchase from one of its sponsors, whose logo appears on the chest of the players.

The avenues of contestation – socio-cultural, politico-economic – that are evident in the spectatorship of the game are directly related to the stadium. Power, identity and fandom are articulated within the material structures supporting the experience of football as a sporting event. The popularity of the game itself thrives on a *topophilia* of the stadium that crosses ideological boundaries.[29] In 'Sports Chatter', Eco devises a test case to illustrate the semiotic and thus codic implications of such a statement in its social and cultural consequences with respect to human behaviour.

You can occupy a cathedral, and you'll have a bishop who protests, some upset Catholics, a fringe of approving dissidents, an indulgent left-wing, the traditional secular parties (secretly) happy. And you can occupy a party's headquarters, and other parties, with or without a show of solidarity, will think it serves them right. But if a stadium is occupied, apart from the immediate reactions, the disclaiming of responsibility would be total: Church, Left, Right, State, Judiciary, Chinese, League for Divorce, anarchist unions, all would send the criminals to the pillory.[30]

The scenario that Eco details in this text (and repeats at the end of 'The World Cup and its Pomps') is quite ridiculous. And he knows it. In fact, he tells us so. 'The very idea sounds ironic and absurd', Eco acknowledges; 'try saying it in public and people will laugh in your face'.[31] Why does he therefore depict the football stadium as a *sacred place* that cuts across spiritual and ideological affiliations? The characterisation hides a provocation that is unsuspectedly radical: to 'discover the inconsistencies of Man as a social animal'.[32] Can we use sports to do that? The short answer is yes. Eco provides the example to expose the extreme psychological and emotional investment that Western society has in the revering of sport and play as a way of human life and of making meaning of experience. Football is only a game. Surely it is not as serious a pursuit as Eco claims? There is embellishment here, and plenty of it, in the above example.

Eco thrives on hyperbole because it parodies reality, exposes its absurdity, and drives the point home with the bludgeoning effect of a hammer. Sport brings about curious allegiances, extreme ideologies, contradictory emotions. It also causes illogical behaviour. People wear the outlandish outfits decorated by the colours of their favourite football team as identifiable markers of a community of worshippers, revere the number of a 'star' player, bet hard-earned wages (they often can't afford to lose) on the outcome of a game, collect such memorabilia as autographs or a sweat-drenched, dis-aromatic jersey, and sometimes lose their lives in violent confrontations with supporters of a hated rival. These are the die-hard football 'fans'. You see their 'passion', Eco observes, every Sunday at the local stadiums where games are played by grown men for delirious amounts of money that the average human being will not see in a lifetime of extended toil and excessive labour. But that is not the only place where football fans become conspicuous consumers of sport. There is also another reason why they do so. Eco confesses a dubious love and admiration for the fatalistic psychological drive of typical football fans:

… I must say that I am not against the passion for soccer. On the contrary, I approve of it and consider it providential. Those crowds of fans, cut down by heart attacks in the grandstands, those referees who pay for a Sunday of fame by personal exposure to grievous bodily harm, those excursionists who climb, bloodstained, from the buses, wounded by shattered glass from windows smashed by stones, those

celebrating young men who speed drunkenly through the streets in the evening, their banner poking from the overloaded Fiat Cinquecento, until they crash into a juggernaut truck, those athletes physically ruined by piercing sexual abstinences, those families financially destroyed after succumbing to insane scalpers [ticket touts], *those enthusiasts whose cannoncrackers explode and blind them: They fill my heart with joy.*[33]

Given the excesses of fanhood that Eco documents – with great relish, I might add – it is surprising that the word 'fan' is now more or less sanitised in the popular vernacular of media culture. Responses to what it signifies about the cultural practices of spectatorship and fandom are ambivalent, if not positive. The negative connotations of fanaticism as an illogical commitment on the part of an individual to a game, sport or activity no longer dominate the semantic field of the word 'fan'. Its positive reclamation has allowed a new set of mental associations to evolve around the cultural politics of the structure of football spectatorship and support, despite all the closed-circuit surveillance cameras, security pens and cages that are now found in major stadiums to keep fanatical activity in check. The following ideological presuppositions characterise the paradigmatic gist of this fresh look at the ethos of fanaticism and its real-world consequences: 'Fans are harmless. Hooligans are not.' In the gregariousness of its social forms of interaction, the *circenses* atmosphere of the stadium that Eco has described 'restrain[s] the uncontrollable energies of the crowd'[34] where the fan activity is mutually beneficent and non-violent, even though alcohol may be used to incite the carnival atmosphere. Songs, chants, eating, heavy drinking, swearing, joking, wearing costumes or stylised garb dominate the boisterous behaviour of watching a game. 'Hooligan' and 'Super-hooligan' are two terms that have come to characterise the negative manifestations of a football identity dedicated to expressing support for a team in ways that promise to spill over into violence. Rivalry is instigated and systematically pursued, no matter what the cost. Social and political conflicts are rolled into the competitive violence enacted between opposing groups of supporters. The aim is to better an equal for the right to claim honour and status within and among rival hooligan 'mob' formations. Violence is not directed towards the public. There is no honour in that. Hooliganism has its own code of acceptable violent behaviour, e.g., conflict must be among willing competitors, weapons are eschewed for fists, the spontaneous engagement of rivals is a priority if at all possible.

If we are to believe Eco, none of this 'sober analysis' matters because the public interest in football is akin to drug addiction or religious rapture, or both, functioning something like the proverbial Marxian opiate for the masses – in which the temperament of fixation most certainly does not depend on logic. On the contrary, it thrives on charismatic mysticism, myth-making and the unencumbered zeal of fanaticism which is driven by *pathos* or passion. To account historically for the global scale of public interest in the World Cup, Eco clarifies how and why the form of spectacle itself does not depend on the quality of the content of the performance or its expression.

There's no need to ask ourselves why the World Cup has so morbidly polarized the attention of the public and the devotion of the mass media: From the famous story of how a comedy by Terence played to an empty house because there was a trained bear show elsewhere, and the acute observation of Roman emperors about the usefulness of circenses, *to the shrewd use that dictatorships (including the Argentinian) have always made of great competitive events ...* [35]

Football, as all sport, produces its own forms of communication that mobilise signs and systems of signs to assemble codes and codic frameworks wherein meaning is made and interpreted. The rules of engagement are a rite of initiation to the exegetic code of the game.

One needs to know them to understand and explain what is happening on the field between the players, regardless of ideology. Football thus produces its own *model reader*, or in this case, the 'model fan'. That is, one who can apprehend, apply and reproduce the cognitive and aesthetic structures at play within the interpretative and performative levels of the game itself, including the text of its discourse. The problem for Eco is not football, *the sport*, but what football and its signifying machinery teaches the fan about relating to the world and, more importantly, to others. The unfortunate reality is that 'athletes are competing in play, but the voyeurs compete seriously (and in fact, they beat up one another or die of heart failure in the grandstands)'.[36]

Talking Football

In his essay 'How Not to Talk About Football',[37] Eco plays with the semiotic dimensions of the discourse that football produces by describing the 'idle talk' or 'chatter' produced by the football fan in conversation with someone who does not want to talk football. Hence, the dual reference of the title, to 'the fan' and to 'the anti-fan' as the subject of the essay. Eco personalises the issue. He 'recognize[s] and appreciate[s] all the merits of this noble sport',[38] but, he explains, 'I hate football fans'.[39] The rationale that Eco gives is analogous to the reason for chauvinism, racism and xenophobia – fear of the difference of the other:

Please do not misunderstand me. My feelings toward fans are exactly those the xenophobes of the Lombard League feel towards immigrants from the Third World. 'I'm not a racist, so long as they stay home.' By 'home' here I mean both the places where they like to gather during the week (bars, living rooms, clubs) and the stadiums, where I am not interested in what happens. And for me it's a plus if the Liverpool fans arrive, because then I can amuse myself reading the news reports: if we must have circenses, *some blood at least should be spilled.*[40]

These comments would be difficult to take for some, considering their lack of political correctness. To all intents and purposes, Eco confesses to actively discriminating against football fans. Looking deeper, the reason is rooted in semiotics, in the forms of communication that he sees football instantiating: 'I don't like the football fan, because he [notice the male pronoun] has a strange defect; he cannot understand why you are not a fan yourself, and he insists on talking to you as if you were.'[41] From an ideological viewpoint, 'the fan' and 'the anti-fan' exist in mutually exclusive and contradictory possible worlds that determine, and are determined by, the individual's own internal construction of external reality. They do not share the same ideo-cultural constructs regarding the way in which football is perceived. There is no common code, *intertext* or *interlanguage* to engage the individuals in a dialogical exchange of information and the subsequent intentional and extentional acts of meaning-making that are required in dyadic communication structures.

Mis-communication is the product of an *aberrant recoding* of signs across codes. The following dialogue between a hypothetical football fan and anti-fan illustrates the point that Eco is making:

'So *what about Vialli, eh?*'

'*I must have missed that.*'

'*But you're going to watch the game tonight, aren't you?*'

'*No, I have to work on Book Z of the Metaphysics, you know? The Stagirite.*'

'*Okay. You watch it and you'll see if I'm right or not. I say Van Basten might be the new Maradona. What do you think? But I'd keep an eye on Aldaiz, all the same.*'[42]

There is no communication going on here – just cross-talk with plenty of ideological interference, and an overcoding of content that reinforces the conceptual distance between the interlocutors. No room is left for the listener to co-reference what each initiating speaker is signifying, thus rendering the input incomprehensible and therefore meaningless. 'Like talking to a wall',[43] Eco says. To be fair, he also takes the air out of his own passion for playing the recorder by giving an example of a similarly one-sided conversation between himself, as an enthusiast of the instrument who uses an ideolect of specialised terms, and someone who doesn't play the recorder and 'doesn't care a fig'.[44] Referring to this hypothetical football fan's mono-genetic and mono-dimensional discourse, Eco surmises:

It isn't that he doesn't care a fig that I don't care a fig. It's that he can't conceive that anyone could exist and not care a fig. He wouldn't understand it even if I had three eyes and a pair of antennae emerging from the green scales of my nape.[45]

The result is *chatter*, *idle talk*, mis- or non-communication. That is, a gratuitous variety of discourse whose efforts at communication are without point or purpose because there is no reciprocally productive exchange of words and concepts. All the signs are overcoded by the illusory expectations of the one participant that the other shares a knowledge of the same code. This presumption is incorrect because it takes a lot for granted, as Eco's comedic example adeptly reveals. Talk that fills up the absurd emptiness of the reality that constitutes the empirical plane of human space and time is governed strictly by conventions, clichés and the *Realpolitik* of divulging personal information as shared experiences and expectations, e.g., what one should say or expects to be said in certain social situations. This chatter lacks imagination, although it is not totally negative.

Communication requires a 'pre-existent language',[46] Eco tells us after Martin Heidegger, a discourse that 'speaks us' – a speaking 'in which we are spoken'.[47] The intimacy of this form of talk – 'phatic speech' in which emotions and feelings are expressed for the sake of expressing them (e.g., 'How are you?' 'I'm fine, thanks') – keeps the possibility of communication open, wherein human relationships and their social institutions are nurtured and can flourish. There is no waste of the potential to recognise the horizons of an other. 'If this function atrophies', Eco states, 'we have constant contact without any message. Like a radio that is turned on but not tuned, so a background noise and some static inform us that we are, indeed, in a kind of communication with something, but the radio doesn't allow us to know anything'.[48] Since the propensity for speech is a human biological trait, the capacity for talk comes quite naturally to us, and its semiogenesis in language is a primary source of social communication.

'Sports activity', Eco declares, is dominated by the idea of 'waste'.[49] But the loss is always counterpoised against a gain measured after the fact. Eco equates the waste of energy on the discourse of football with the action of sport as it tends towards entropy, or movement towards the lowest point of energy, *stasis*. A moral hierarchy that ensnares both spectators and players is implied by the loss of vitality. The ethical dimensions of what is lost and gained begin to map out the boundaries of human relationships within the sporting world and beyond it. In Italy, for example, fan allegiances construct and reinforce the political sphere and class structure of that country. Italy's richest man, media magnate and Prime Minister Silvio Berlusconi owns AC Milan. Fans of the club are generally supporters of the Forza Italia party to which Berlusconi belongs. Juventus, owned by the founders of Fiat, the Agnelli family, is a symbol of wealth, while workers on the Fiat assembly line prefer Torino. It would not be overstating the case to say that a politician's chances for election may well be enhanced or diminished by well-established football loyalties. Why else would Berlusconi postpone a Derby scheduled between AC Milan and Inter Milan (an inner-city rival) on election day, if not to make sure that all the AC Milan football fans voted, presumably for the Forza Italia party?

Sport translates into politics via discourse and, in this case, football culture. Eco calls this 'sport cubed'[50] because it is discussion generated from the spectatorship of sport 'as something seen',[51] or 'sport squared (which involves speculation and barter, selling and enforced consumption)'.[52] Sports talk comes to be a surrogate speech for disputation about politics. That is not always an undesirable thing, as Eco avers in 'The World Cup and its Pomps'. This essay was written in 1978 during the atmosphere of angst fulminating around the Red Brigades' reign of terror.[53] He says that the writing of this text was a temporary relief from the escalating tensions caused by the kidnapping of Aldo Moro and other acts of politically motivated terrorism that dominated Italian media coverage at the time, feeding public concerns over national security. Eco decries the spectacle, yet admits that the pomp of the World Cup provided a brief distraction for the country and quelled thoughts about the spectre of violence as a real threat to the safety of all citizens: 'But since external pressure impels me to reflect, I might as well say that public opinion, especially in Italy, has never needed a nice international championship more than it does now.'[54] Competitive sport holds the power to consolidate the boundaries of local and regional, national and international borders, and give an identity to difference on a global scale.

Eco realises the necessity of play to the mental well-being of the human animal. Games provide a release of pent-up energy via recourse to a 'recreational waste'.[55] The 'physical and psychic need for play'[56] is a manifestation of the human inability to cope with mundane forms of repetition and closed systems that offer no immediate openings for change. Withstanding the *ennui* of routine depends on the existence of an imaginary world of play whose rules are outside the strict institutional structures of labour. 'Being free', in this sense, is the 'freeing ourselves from the tyranny of indispensable work'[57] – even if it is a vicarious play lived through the viewing of the minds and bodies of others in play. Eco derogatorily calls spectators of professional sports 'voyeurs'. Football fans are even worse. But the imagination of the viewer still involves the mind and the body in the phenomenality of its escape route, whether good or bad. *Homo ludens*, in the proper sense, is 'man' at play, exercising and transforming the gifts of nature bestowed upon human beings. By 'proper sense', I mean, as Eco does, 'in which one person, with no financial incentive, and employing his [or her] own body directly, performs physical exercises'.[58]

The social and cultural impact of a World Cup is not the athletic prowess that the players exhibit to enthusiasts and aficionados of the game, but the chance that a country has to display and claim itself and its people as *the* universal champions, for four years at least. Along with the 'survival of the fittest' mentality, promoted at a global sporting event and its competitive tournaments structure, comes the bravado of phatic speech, animated debate of unqualified emotion and the public contestation for 'bragging rights' – the right to claim categorical superiority of one nation over another by measuring human aptitude in relation to facility at a set of game skills – like how many times a ball can be kicked into the back of a goal. Talk naturally accompanies the political imperative of an international athletic event such as the World Cup for no other reason than that speculation fuels the production of language and is consequently an expression of human commitment to the 'glorification of Waste, and therefore the maximum point of Consumption'.[59]

A 'continuous phatic discourse that deceitfully passes itself off as talk of the City and its Ends'[60] is Eco's definition of sports chatter. In it, he identifies the self-directed and autotelic nature of the terms of expression. Sports chatter is a discourse that refers to itself and the internal circumstances of its production. Its ideological purpose to display emotion becomes a motivating end in itself, like venting to show displeasure. The passion of sports chatter is the zenith of solipsism, Eco argues, given that the situational premises of the discourse are self-serving and thus critically vapid: 'On it and in it every consumer civilization man actually consumes himself (and every possibility of thematizing and judging the enforced consumption to which he is invited and subjected).'[61] The commodification of football could not happen without the fanaticism of the talk revolving around its signifying practices. 'Sports talk' becomes 'sports chatter' when the 'illusion of interest in sport'[62] can be made to seem real and 'the notion of *practicing* sport becomes confused with *talking sport*; the chatterer thinks himself an athlete and is no longer aware that he doesn't engage in sport'.[63] The hallucination is shared because it is produced *en masse* and perpetuated on the sports talk shows, where the discourse is catalysed not essentially by the sport *itself*, but by the *talk of sport* and the *reporting* of it within the media.

Eco comes to the conclusion that sport today consists of 'discussion of the sports press',[64] which is a 'discourse on a discourse about watching others' sport as discourse'.[65] He goes on to suggest that, in 1968:

If through some diabolical machination of the Mexican government and chairman Avery Brundage, in agreement with all the TV networks in the world, the Olympics were not to take place, but were narrated daily and hourly through fictitious images, nothing in the international sports system would change, nor would the sports discussants feel cheated.[66]

The phatic structure of the communication subverts even the possibility that the vehicle for debate might be a faked scenario. Like the tail wagging the dog, sports chatter as a 'disquisition on play'[67] allows the speaker to discourse like an expert on the subject while accepting no *real* responsibility for the ideas and attitudes expressed, even if – or perhaps especially because – the circumstances of utterance are grounded in *simulations of reality* and not empirical occurrences. Sports talk allows the speaker 'to take positions, express opinions, suggest solutions'[68] with no fear of retribution by the powers that be, since the topic of discussion is 'beyond the area of the speaker's power'.[69] There is no contingent possibility for the fan as a speaking subject to intervene either in the field of sporting activity where the game is played or in its corridors of power. Sports chatter presupposes irresponsibility via the form of the speaker's engaged detachment while playing the role of commentator-cum-inquisitor. Energy is expended towards an 'empty discussion'[70] in which ignorance is total and hidden behind a façade of the subject's total immersion in phatic speech for the sake of impassioned expression. Psychologically, to the adult male who is the primary consumer of professional sport, especially football, Eco declares, 'it's like little girls playing ladies: a pedagogical game, which teaches you how to occupy your proper place'.[71]

Sports chatter is then 'the easiest substitute for political debate',[72] because the nature of the discourse is still all about the ability to wield power and dominance over others while uttering opinions that are a 'total falsification of every political attitude'.[73] Subjective agency is put on hold. Engaging in sports chatter requires specialised knowledge, but it allows you 'to play at the direction of government without all the sufferings, the duties, the imponderables of political debate'[74] and the psychological consequences of legislating on behalf of others. For this reason, Eco is of the belief that 'sport fulfils its role of fake conscience'[75] by allowing the citizen to participate in public discussion without having to act in a way that genuinely engages others through dialogue or action about the social sphere. The critical movements of political debate are mimicked in sports chatter as parallel forms of social engagement:

Instead of judging the job done by the minister of finance (for which you have to know about economics, among other things), you discuss the job done by the coach; instead of criticizing the record of Parliament you criticize the record of the athletes; instead of asking (difficult and obscure question) if such-and-such a minister signed some shady agreements with such-and-such a foreign power, you ask if the final or decisive game will be decided by chance, by athletic prowess, or by diplomatic alchemy.[76]

This is disturbing for Eco, given that professional football has nothing to offer society for renewal beyond 'the parody of political talk'.[77] The ritual of sports chatter in the public sphere allays the social guilt of the citizen by offering the opportunity to engage and participate in a universal 'democratic' polemics with others, but not for the betterment of society. The waste of energy is achieved through intellectual exchange and not physical play, yet it is still a waste of the possibility for the citizen's intervention into the realm of the political occupying the public sphere.

Concluding on the Sign of Football

We must remember that for Eco, sporting activity can be divided into two categories: sports for health and recreation and sports for competition and money. The rise of play as competition is what differentiates between a 'profoundly healthy waste'[78] and a contestation of skills in which the game and its rules 'reduce innate aggressiveness to a system, brute force to intelligence'.[79] The distinction still depends on the waste of energy, Eco maintains, whether a stone is flung for 'sheer pleasure' or to 'aim to fling one still farther'[80] than another, since every sport is predicated on the notion of escaping and freeing oneself from the drudgery of labour and its social and ideological institutions. Intelligence is spent in the transformation of spontaneous, autopoietic play into a contest in which a code of play provides the rules of engagement against which the competitors struggle and are measured by themselves and by others. Football is a game of goals and tactics, strategies of attack and defensive formations. The teams play against each other, and skill determines the outcome to varying degrees on any given match day, but ultimately the contest is waged against and within the rules of engagement and the clock, fought according to the codic parameters of the 'laws of football'. Otherwise, why would a referee be required to mediate the competition and 'control the competitive spirit'?[81] The game would go on without the necessity for a sanctioned gatekeeper to level the playing field, so to speak, and keep the players honest to each other and the rules of the game. Theoretically, there would be less controversy and much less need for the 'verbal rituals'[82] that would shift sports chatter on football to another plane where it would resemble 'political' discourse. On the one hand, the form and content of sports chatter would be a 'parody of political talk'.[83] As Eco states, it is concerned with 'what the leaders should have done, what they did do, what we would have liked them to do, what happened, and what will happen'.[84] On the other hand, 'in this parody the strength that the citizen had at his disposal for political debate is vitiated and disciplined'.[85]

Because of this ethical dimension of speech as performance, Eco can go further. He calls sports chatter the 'ersatz of political speech, but to such a heightened degree that it becomes itself political speech'.[86] The ramifications of sport as competition affect the socio-political sphere of the subject, but not in a way that we would expect: 'Contest disciplines and neutralizes the aggressive charge, individual and collective. It reduces excess action, but it is really a mechanism to neutralize action.'[87] Defusing resistance comes to be the ethos of a community. The systematic waste of energy, both positive and negative, does become translated into physical and intellectual gain, since '[r]aces improve the race'.[88] However, there is a degeneration of health and of the contest that is the result of the singular drive to better the other at sport and then to chatter about it.

Coming back to the original question, 'What does the sign of "football" signify?', with respect to sports and its chatter, it is 'A place of total ignorance',[89] Umberto Eco concludes. Football spawns cultural practices of fan behaviour that are a 'falsification of every political attitude',[90] despite the call to action which they convey in the name of freedom of speech and action. So, 'no political summons'[91] could affect the production of sports chatter and the conspicuous consumption of the sign of the game on the field and off. Football is played with the City and its inhabitants in mind. Its signs are meaningful only insofar as they relate to the production of a spectator culture whose empirical identities coincide with well-established allegiances that exist within an alter ego or subjectivity that we can call 'the fan'. When the sign of football crosses over, in the fan, from reality to discourse – and Eco maintains that it can never be anything but discourse disguised as 'sports talk' – the point of communication becomes the expression of desire through free and uncensored speech. An inalienable right. Politics defines the semiotic space of the game, its representational milieu, and how the fan relates to it on a personal level, with, and through, others. The sign of football produces the media machine and also creates the need for it. 'Thus', Eco says, 'no revolutionary would have the courage to revolutionize the availability for sports chatter'.[92] For this would mean circumventing the right to freedom of expression: '[T]he citizen would take over the protest, transforming its slogans into sports chatter, or suddenly rejecting, and with desperate distrust, the intrusion of reason in his reasonable exercise of highly rational verbal rules.'[93]

If anything, football as a sport is a signifier whose historicity acts as a stabilising agent upon cultural memory in that it refers to a common thread of logic, of which we spoke at the beginning of this book: 'Sport is Man, Sport is Society.' Attempting to arrest the associations between sport, humanity and society (arising from this maxim) that have percolated throughout Western culture – and have spawned it – is akin to attempting to bring down the ethical and conceptual foundations of Western civic society and democracy. Who would want to bear the responsibility and the stigma for that? That is why, Umberto Eco affirms, no revolutionary group, no matter how radical, would ever occupy the field on a football Sunday.

Notes

1. Umberto Eco, *A Theory of Semiotics*, Bloomington: Indiana University Press, 1976, p. 28.

2. Ibid., p. 28.

3. Umberto Eco, *The Role of the Reader: Explorations in the Semiotics of Texts*, Bloomington: Indiana University Press, 1979.

4. Umberto Eco, 'The World Cup and its Pomps', in *Travels in Hyper Reality*, trans. William Weaver, New York and London: Harcourt Brace & Company, 1986, p. 172.

5. Eco, *A Theory of Semiotics*, p. 7.

6. Umberto Eco, 'Sports Chatter', in *Travels in Hyper Reality*, op. cit., p. 159.

7. Eco, 'The World Cup and its Pomps', p. 169.

8. See Gary Armstrong and Richard Giulianoti (eds), *Entering the Field*, Oxford: Berg, 1997, for a more detailed analysis of the ideological code switching of the Aberdeen fans.

9. See Eco, *A Theory of Semiotics*, pp. 286–98.

10. Eco, 'Sports Chatter', p. 160.

11. Ibid., p. 160.

12. Ibid., p. 160.

13. Ibid., p. 160.

14. Ibid., p. 160.

15. Eco, 'The World Cup and its Pomps', p. 167.

16. Ibid., p. 167.

17. Ibid., p. 168.

18. Ibid., p. 168.

19. Ibid., p. 168.

20. Ibid., p. 168.

21. Ibid., p. 168.

22. Ibid., p. 168.

23. Fighting between Liverpool and Juventus supporters during the 1985 European Cup Final at the Heysel Stadium in Brussels resulted in the death of 39 people, and the subsequent banning of English football clubs from European competitions for five years.

24. Eco, 'The World Cup and its Pomps', p. 169.

25. Eco, 'Sports Chatter', p. 160.

26. Ibid., p. 160.

27. Ibid., p. 161.

28. See Eco, *A Theory of Semiotics*, pp. 48–150.

29. See Richard Giulianoti, *Football: A Sociology of the Game*, Malden, MA: Polity Press, 1999.

30. Eco, 'Sports Chatter', p. 160.

31. Ibid., p. 159.

32. Ibid., p. 160.

33. Eco, 'The World Cup and its Pomps', pp. 168–9.

34. Eco, 'Sports Chatter', p. 162.

35. Eco, 'The World Cup and its Pomps', p. 170.

36. Eco, 'Sports Chatter', p. 162.

37. The essay is translated in *Travels in Hyper Reality* as 'How Not to Talk About Soccer'. For the sake of continuity, I have changed the word 'soccer' to 'football' when citing it from this essay.

38. Umberto Eco, 'How Not to Talk About Football', in *Travels in Hyper Reality*, op. cit., p. 39.

39. Ibid., p. 39.

40. Ibid., p. 39.

41. Ibid., pp. 39–40.

42. Ibid., p. 41.

43. Ibid., p. 41.

44. Ibid., p. 41.

45. Ibid., p. 41.

46. Eco, 'Sports Chatter', p. 164.

47. Ibid., p. 164.

48. Ibid., pp. 164–5.

49. Ibid., p. 160.

50. Ibid., p. 162.

51. Ibid., p. 162.

52. Ibid., p. 162.

53. The Red Brigades were a group of terrorists operating in Italy during the late 1970s. They kidnapped

and eventually killed former Italian Prime Minister Aldo Moro.

54. Eco, 'The World Cup and its Pomps', p. 170.

55. Eco, 'Sports Chatter', p. 160.

56. Ibid., p. 160.

57. Ibid., p. 160.

58. Eco, 'The World Cup and its Pomps', p. 168.

59. Eco, 'Sports Chatter', p. 165.

60. Ibid., p. 165.

61. Ibid., p. 165.

62. Ibid., p. 163.

63. Ibid., p. 163.

64. Ibid., p. 162.

65. Ibid., p. 162.

66. Ibid., p. 162.

67. Ibid., p. 161.

68. Eco, 'The World Cup and its Pomps', p. 171.

69. Ibid., p. 171.

70. Eco, 'Sports Chatter', p. 165.

71. Eco, 'The World Cup and its Pomps', p. 171.

72. Ibid., p. 170.

73. Eco, 'Sports Chatter', p. 165.

74. Eco, 'The World Cup and its Pomps', p. 171.

75. Eco, 'Sports Chatter', p. 163.

76. Eco, 'The World Cup and its Pomps', p. 171.

77. Eco, 'Sports Chatter', p. 163.
78. Ibid., p. 160.
79. Ibid., p. 161.
80. Ibid., p. 160.
81. Ibid., p. 161.
82. Ibid., p. 163.
83. Ibid., p. 163.
84. Ibid., p. 163.
85. Ibid., p. 163.
86. Ibid., p. 163.
87. Ibid., p. 161.
88. Ibid., p. 161.
89. Ibid., p. 165.
90. Ibid., p. 165.
91. Ibid., p. 165.
92. Ibid., p. 165.
93. Ibid., p. 165.

Select Bibliography

Umberto Eco, *The Aesthetics of Thomas Aquinas*, Cambridge, MA: Harvard University Press, 1954

Umberto Eco, *A Theory of Semiotics*, Bloomington: Indiana University Press, 1976

Umberto Eco, *The Role of the Reader: Explorations in the Semiotics of Texts*, Bloomington: Indiana University Press, 1979

Umberto Eco, *The Name of the Rose*, trans. William Weaver, New York: Secker and Warburg, 1980

Umberto Eco, *Semiotics and the Philosophy of Language*, Bloomington: Indiana University Press, 1984

Umberto Eco, *Interpretation and Overinterpretation*, Cambridge: Cambridge University Press, 1992

Umberto Eco, *Misreadings*, trans. William Weaver, London: Jonathan Cape, 1993

Umberto Eco, *Six Walks in the Fictional Woods*, Cambridge, MA: Harvard University Press, 1994

Umberto Eco, *Kant and the Platypus: Essays on Language and Cognition*, trans. Alastair McEwen, New York: Harcourt Brace & Company, 2000

Key Ideas and Glossary

Agon

The word '*agon*' comes from the Greek *agonas* which means titanic struggle, battle or competition. English words such as 'agony' and 'protagonist' are derived from *agon*, which signifies the anxiety of going head-to-head against an agent of opposition.

Autopoietic

Autopoietic joins the Greek words *auto*, which means the thing in itself (e.g., the subject), and *poietic*, which is derived from *poiesis*, to make. Autopoietic therefore means 'making itself, by its own means of production'

Autotelic

Autotelic is a compound word joining two Greek words: *auto*, the thing in itself (e.g., the subject), and *telic*, which is a version of *telos*, or end. Autotelic therefore means 'looking to itself for meaning as the end of all things'.

Hermeneutical

Hermeneutics is a philosophical school of interpretation that has its roots in phenomenological inquiry regarding the existence and meaning of objects in relation to a subject's perceptions of them. 'Hermeneutical' has come to describe the application of principles of interpretation to a text or context.

Images and Icons

According to semiotics, there are five classes of images: 1) *graphic* (pictures, statues, designs); 2) *optical* (mirrors, projections); 3) *perceptual* (sense data); 4) *mental* (dreams, memories, ideas); 5) *verbal* (metaphor, descriptions). The traditional semiotic definition of an image is rooted in distinguishing its features based on resemblance to the object being represented. The concept of image defined as resemblance, however, refers to 'visual' phenomena and their mental representations. It does not cover a broader spectrum of sign production including transmission through non-visual channels (e.g., spoken language). An image becomes an icon when its properties are similar to what it refers to. For example, a crucifix becomes an icon because its shape and form retain the character and geometrical properties of the original crucifix referred to in the Bible story of Jesus Christ. The representation of the crucifix does not depend on anything other than itself here, because it signifies and represents itself.

Intentional/Extentional responses

Intentional responses are consciously motivated acts of meaning-making that the reader/viewer performs; *extentional* acts are not consciously motivated.

Interpretant

An interpretant is the mental tool or image used to represent an object or a concept to the self. It facilitates understanding.

Lexical

Lexical refers to the representation of concepts using the signs of language, e.g., speech or words.

Phatic

Phatic refers to the statements that express internal emotion or feelings.

Signs and Sign-Functions

The 'sign' presupposes a mental differentiation between a *signifier* (such as a word) and the *signified* (such as an object or thing in reality). Signs are not 'things' or 'objects' but correlations between expression and content, so that we are essentially concerned with sign-*functions* instead of signs. A sign-function occurs when a certain expression is correlated to a particular context; these correlations are culturally created, thus implying artificiality or convention. A language is a convention of signs used for communication. According to this definition of the sign and its functions, there are no universal truths because meaning is not fixed and is often provisionally bound in culturally-determined semantic fields. For example, a sign-function operates in every lie to signify something not of, or not true to, the external world. For example, if I begin a story with 'Once upon a time there was a flying elephant', then you would know that I was using signs to function in a special way to tell a fairy tale or a make-believe story. The given code of fact versus fiction enables the interpreter to understand sign-functions that are false. Ultimately, the content of an expression is not an object but a cultural unit. There are no such things as flying elephants. If we know the proper code of correlations between expression and content, we can understand how signs are being used. Language, then, is a semiotic system embodying artificial and conventional sign-meaning correlations.

Structuralism and Semiotics

A 'methodological structuralism' is a programme for reading and decoding texts. As Umberto Eco maintains in *The Role of the Reader: Explorations in the Semiotics of Texts* (1979), structuralism provides a language of criticism without which there would be no way to achieve the purpose(s) of semiological inquiry relevant to the examination of meaning-making. A semiotic method of textual analysis is accordingly considered to encompass means or devices (e.g., a metalanguage, a 'model', figures or other visual schemata, etc.) that conceptualise in *hypothetical* rather than *real* terms the acts of meaning-making that a reader or viewer engages in relative to the structures of signification comprising a text. There are *intentional* responses or consciously motivated acts of meaning-making that the reader/viewer performs, and *extentional* acts that are not consciously motivated.

Syntagmatic

A syntagm is a unit of meaning that is complete in itself, such as a phrase, a sentence, a paragraph, a narrative text, etc.

Text and Textuality

The term 'text' has evoked various meanings according to particular disciplinary perspectives. In cognitive psychology, it has been represented as the sum of propositions put forward by an author in a variety of forms and genres; in semiotics, as the set of lexical or visual signs that act as 'cues' to guide the reader's inbuilt disposition for mental decoding operations. Structuralist theorists after Ferdinand de Saussure determined the text to be an object endowed with precise properties that must be analytically isolated, and on the grounds of which the text can be entirely defined. Some proponents of structuralist theorising like Julia Kristeva and Roland Barthes have conceived of 'textuality' as the equivalent of the author's productivity – a polyphony of voices realised via the social exchange of thought. Such a text encapsulates the tensions of knowledge, power and desire that govern human life. Others, like Umberto Eco and Jacques Derrida, have cultivated a conception of text/uality in which meaning-making on the part of the reader is considered to be a creative and playful act of associations that continue to infinity in relation to a seemingly uncontrollable labyrinth of possible interpretations.

Topophilia

Topophilia joins two Greek words: *topos*, which means space or place, and *filia*, which means love. So topophilia is the love of a space or place – in this case, the love of the football stadium.